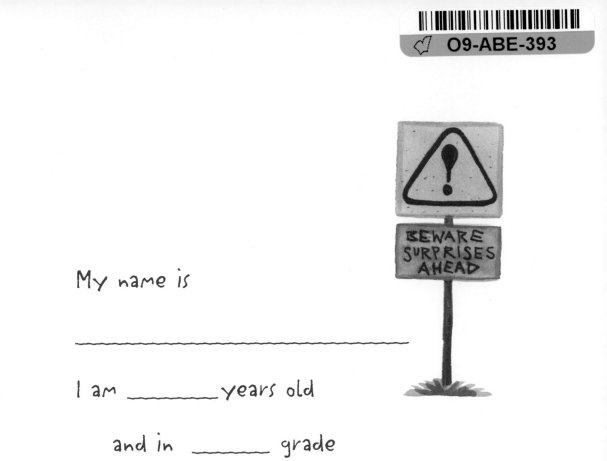

My name is

_____

I am _____ years old

and in _____ grade

My best friend is

_____

I live in Ohio: yes   no

I have lived here for_____

Sleeping Bear Press™

315 E. Eisenhower Parkway, Suite 200
Ann Arbor MI 48108
www.sleepingbearpress.com

Sleeping Bear Press is an imprint of Gale, a part of Cengage Learning.

10 9 8 7 6 5 4 3 2 1

ISBN 978-1-58536-540-1

Printed by China Translation & Printing Services Limited, Guangdong Province, China. 1st printing.   07/2010

Diary of an Ohio Kid

Artwork by Cyd Moore

Where do you live in Ohio?

Your address, town/city, and phone number:

_____

_____

_____

Can you walk to school from your house?

_____

_____

How far away from you do your friends live?

_____

_____

Do you have any parks nearby?

_____

_____

Your favorite thing about your neighborhood is:

_____

_____

_____

CANADA

Michigan

Lake Erie

Toledo

Bowling Green

Sandusky

Cleveland

Youngstown

Akron

Findlay

Ohio

N

Dayton

★Columbus

Athens

Chillicothe

Cincinnati

Portsmouth

Kentucky

Where Do YOU Live?

WRITE!

Today's date: _____

DRAW!

Today's date: _____

The great state of Ohio!

Are you an Ohio kid?
How many state facts do
you already know? See if you
can fill in the right answers!

(The correct answers are at the bottom on the next page.)

State animal:

_____

State bird:

_____

State reptile:

_____

State insect:

_____

State wildflower:

_____

State tree:

State fruit:

State beverage:

State gemstone:

State nickname:

WRITE!

Today's date: _____

_____

_____

_____

_____

_____

_____

_____

_____

_____

_____

_____

_____

_____

_____

_____

_____

DRAW!

Today's date: _____

Today we went to

My favorite thing about today was

My least favorite thing about today was

_____

_____

_____

_____

_____

_____

_____

Would I visit here again? Why or why not?

_____

_____

_____

_____

WRITE!

Today's date: _____

_____

_____

_____

_____

_____

_____

_____

_____

_____

_____

_____

_____

_____

_____

_____

_____

DRAW!

Today's date: _____

Ohioans love their tomatoes!

Did you know that Ohio has a state beverage? Tomato juice! And it's made from Ohio's state fruit—the tomato.

Visit farmer's markets and tomato festivals around the state when tomatoes are in season. See how many different varieties of tomatoes you can find. And when you bring your bounty home, how about making your own salsa!

Ingredients:
- 2 cups chopped tomatoes
- 1 small can diced green chiles
- ¼ cup sliced green onions
- ¼ cup chopped fresh cilantro
- 2 tablespoons lime juice
- 1 clove minced garlic
- salt and pepper to taste

Directions:
Combine ingredients. Cover and chill several hours.

What other recipes can you create with tomatoes? Crush tomatoes for soup or sauce, or make juice for drinking.

What is your
favorite tomato recipe?

_____

_____

_____

_____

_____

_____

_____

_____

WRITE!

Today's date: _____

DRAW!

Today's date: _____

Ohioans take flight!

Orville and Wilbur Wright grew up in Dayton, Ohio. They ran a bicycle shop in Dayton, where they first began experimenting with aviation. The brothers built and flew the first motor-powered airplane in 1903.

By the 1960s we were already flying spaceships, and in 1969 Neil Armstrong became the first man to walk on the moon. He was born in Wapakoneta, Ohio.

Have you ever flown in a plane?

_____

_____

What do you think it'd be like to fly in a space ship?

_____

_____

Make your own paper airplane!

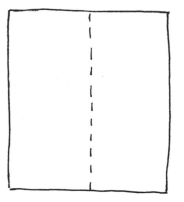

1. Fold paper in half.

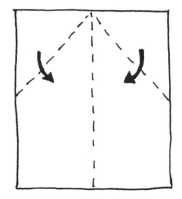

2. Fold top corners down.

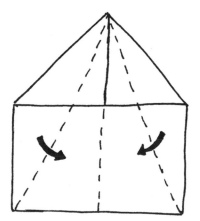

3 Fold paper down on each side.

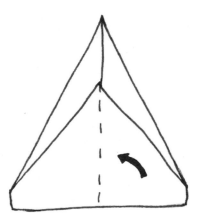

4 Fold in half along center line.

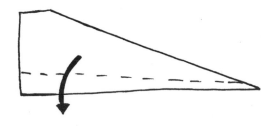

5 Fold sides down in opposite directions.

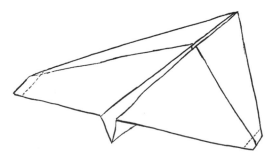
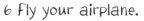

6 Fly your airplane.

WRITE!

Today's date: _____

_____

_____

_____

_____

_____

_____

_____

_____

_____

_____

_____

_____

_____

_____

_____

_____

DRAW!

Today's date: _____

Let's play some games!

Going on a trip?

Here are some fun games to play on your next road trip.

Scavenger Hunt

Before you start out on your trip, make a list of items and places you might see along the way (11 blue cars, 2 bridges, 5 motels, 3 towns that start with the letter M, etc.). Check them off as you find them.

What is the funniest town name you've ever heard?

_____

_____

_____

_____

_____

If you were going to name a town, what would it be?

_____

_____

License Plate Game

Make a list of all the states. See how many different state license plates you can find, and check them off your list.
(Variation: Keep a list of all the vanity plates you find.)

Make up your own funny license plates.

Auto Tag

Each person chooses a symbol or something you are likely to encounter regularly on the road, such as a gas station logo, a restaurant sign, a farm animal, a motorcycle. When a player sees her item, she calls it out and gently tags the next player, who then proceeds to search for his symbol, and so on.

WRITE!

Today's date: _____

_____

_____

_____

_____

_____

_____

_____

_____

_____

_____

_____

_____

_____

_____

_____

DRAW!

Today's date: _____

Today we went to

_____

_____

_____

_____

_____

My favorite thing about today was

_____

_____

_____

_____

_____

_____

_____

_____

_____

_____

My least favorite thing about today was

_____

_____

_____

_____

_____

_____

_____

Would I visit here again? Why or why not?

_____

_____

_____

_____

_____

WRITE!

Today's date: _____

_____

_____

_____

_____

_____

_____

_____

_____

_____

_____

_____

_____

_____

_____

_____

_____

DRAW!

Today's date: _____

Let's GROW something!

Grow a Pizza Garden!

Start plants indoors in early spring, then transfer to pots or the ground outside once they've sprouted and there is no longer danger of frost.

You'll need to grow:

HERBS:

- basil and oregano

VEGETABLES for SAUCE and TOPPINGS:

- tomatoes and bell peppers

What is your very favorite kind of pizza?

...Now...Let's COOK something!

Making a homemade pizza!

FOR YOUR CRUST:

You can use your favorite pizza-dough recipe, or a store-bought pizza crust, or even English muffin halves or tortillas for your crust.

MAKING FRESH PIZZA SAUCE:

Wash and cut as many tomatoes as you like into chunks.
Wash and dry a good handful each of basil and oregano, and chop.

In a saucepan over medium heat, sauté chopped onion and garlic in a small amount of butter or vegetable oil. If you like your sauce spicy, add crushed red pepper next. Now add the tomatoes and herbs and allow the mixture to come to a boil. Turn down the heat to a simmer, stirring occasionally, and let the sauce simmer until most of the liquid has cooked out.

Take sauce off the stove and use either a container blender or a hand-held blender to purée the sauce. Put sauce back on the heat, let it come to a boil again, then allow to simmer until it is the consistency you like.

Let it cool, then spread on pizza dough, or store in the fridge for another time.

ASSEMBLING YOUR PIZZA:

Spread sauce over pizza dough. Top with your chopped, fresh-picked peppers, and any other fresh veggies or meats you like. Now sprinkle cheese over everything and bake in the oven according to your pizza dough recipe. Yum! A home-grown pizza!

WRITE!

Today's date: _____

_____

_____

_____

_____

_____

_____

_____

_____

_____

_____

_____

_____

_____

_____

_____

DRAW!

Today's date: _____

When it rains, my favorite things to do:

_____

_____

_____

_____

_____

_____

_____

_____

_____

_____

Favorite movie

_____

_____

_____

Favorite TV show

_____

_____

_____

Favorite video game

_____

_____

_____

Favorite book

_____

_____

_____

Favorite art projects

_____

_____

_____

WRITE!

Today's date: _____

_____

_____

_____

_____

_____

_____

_____

_____

_____

_____

_____

_____

_____

_____

_____

_____

DRAW!

Today's date: _____

Today we went to

_____

_____

_____

_____

_____

My favorite thing about today was

_____

_____

_____

_____

_____

_____

_____

_____

_____

My least favorite thing about today was

Would I visit here again? Why or why not?

WRITE!

Today's date: _____

DRAW!

Today's date: _____

Today we went to

_____

_____

_____

_____

My favorite thing about today was

_____

_____

_____

_____

_____

_____

_____

_____

_____

_____

My least favorite thing about today was

_____

_____

_____

_____

_____

_____

_____

Would I visit here again? Why or why not?

_____

_____

_____

_____

_____

_____

_____

WRITE!

Today's date: _____

_____

_____

_____

_____

_____

_____

_____

_____

_____

_____

_____

_____

_____

_____

_____

_____

_____

_____

DRAW!

Today's date: _____

Let's play MORE GAMES!

Billboard Poetry

1. Take turns choosing four words from road signs.
2. Give those words to another player who will have one minute to turn the words into a four-line rhyming poem using one word per line.

Eating the Alphabet Game

To start, the first player says, "I'm so hungry I could eat an apple" (or anteater, or alligator). The second player then has to choose something beginning with the next letter of the alphabet, adding to the first player's choice: "I'm so hungry I could eat an apple and a balloon," and so on. See if your family can make it to Z, with each player remembering all the items that came before: "apple, balloon…zebra!"

What is your favorite food?

_____

_____

_____

_____

Can you think of some of your
own fun games to play?

_____
_____
_____
_____
_____
_____
_____
_____

WRITE!

Today's date: _____

_____

_____

_____

_____

_____

_____

_____

_____

_____

_____

_____

_____

_____

_____

_____

DRAW!

Today's date: _____

Today we went to

_____

_____

_____

_____

My favorite thing about today was

_____

_____

_____

_____

_____

_____

_____

_____

My least favorite thing about today was

_____

_____

_____

_____

_____

_____

_____

Would I visit here again? Why or why not?

_____

_____

_____

_____

_____

_____

WRITE!

Today's date: _____

DRAW!

Today's date: _____

Let's go CAMPING!

Have you ever gone camping? You can go camping in your own backyard. If it's too cold to camp outside, how about camping in your living room? You can even make s'mores in the kitchen oven!

Write about your camping experiences, or where you hope to go camping someday.

_____

_____

_____

_____

_____

_____

_____

Outside and Inside S'mores

You'll need

Marshmallows
Graham crackers, broken in halves
Chocolate bars, broken in halves
A long stick or skewer for campfire s'mores, or
a baking sheet and aluminum foil for indoor s'mores

HOW TO MAKE CAMPFIRE S'MORES

Get your graham crackers and chocolate ready first.
Lay a chocolate bar half on one graham cracker half and have another
graham cracker half ready to go. Now put a marshmallow on the end of
your stick and hold over the fire, turning to keep it browning nicely and
evenly on all sides. It's finished when it's brown all over and a little crispy
on the outside. Now have a friend sandwich the marshmallow between
the graham and chocolate halves while you pull your stick out of the
marshmallow. Now you have a s'more!

HOW TO MAKE S'MORES IN THE OVEN

Heat oven to 350 degrees. Line a baking sheet with foil. Lay cracker halves
on baking sheet, top with chocolate bar halves, then marshmallows. Toast in
oven for about 5 minutes, just until marshmallow is melty and chocolate
begins to soften. Remove from oven and top with another graham cracker
half. S'mores indoors all year round!

WRITE!

Today's date: _____

DRAW!

Today's date: _____

When I grow up I want to be

_____

_____

_____

_____

_____

_____

_____

_____

_____

_____

_____

_____

A place I hope to go someday

WRITE!

Today's date: _____

_____

_____

_____

_____

_____

_____

_____

_____

_____

_____

_____

_____

_____

_____

_____

DRAW!

Today's date: _____

If I wrote a book it would be about

_____

_____

_____

_____

_____

_____

_____

_____

_____

If I made a movie, it would be about

_____

_____

If I made a TV show, it would be about

_____

_____

If I could star in a movie, I would star as a

_____

_____

If I could star in a TV show, I would star as a

_____

_____

I think it would be fun to be an actor because

_____

_____

WRITE!

Today's date: _____

DRAW!

Today's date: _____

Today we went to

_____

_____

_____

_____

My favorite thing about today was

_____

_____

_____

_____

_____

_____

_____

_____

_____

My least favorite thing about today was

Would I visit here again? Why or why not?

WRITE!

Today's date: _____

_____

_____

_____

_____

_____

_____

_____

_____

_____

_____

_____

_____

_____

_____

_____

_____

DRAW!

Today's date: _____

What do you love about going back to school?

School days

My favorite subject in school

_____

_____

_____

My least favorite subject in school

_____

_____

_____

If I were a teacher, I would

_____

_____

_____

If I could change one thing about school, I would

_____

_____

_____

The thing I like most about school

_____

_____

_____

WRITE!

Today's date: _____

_____

_____

_____

_____

_____

_____

_____

_____

_____

_____

_____

_____

_____

_____

_____

_____

WRITE!

Today's date: _____

_____

_____

_____

_____

_____

_____

_____

_____

_____

_____

_____

_____

_____

_____

_____

_____

DRAW!

Today's date: _____

A place I hope to go someday

_____

_____

_____

If I could live anywhere in the world I'd choose

_____

_____

_____

Someone I wish lived near me

_____

_____

_____

Of all the places I've been, I liked this place best

_____

_____

_____

Of all the places I've been, I really didn't like

_____

_____

_____

If I could change one thing
about where I live it would be

_____

_____

_____

_____

_____

_____

_____

_____

WRITE!

Today's date: _____

_____

_____

_____

_____

_____

_____

_____

_____

_____

_____

_____

_____

_____

_____

_____

_____

_____

DRAW!

Today's date: _____

Can you write your own poem? Here's how.

1st Stanza

I am.. *(two special characteristics you have)*

I wonder .... *(something you are actually curious about)*

I hear .... *(an imaginary sound)*

I see... *(an imaginary sight)*

I want.. *(an actual desire)*

I am.. *(the first line of the poem repeated)*

2nd Stanza

I pretend .... *(something you actually pretend to do)*

I feel .... *(a feeling about something imaginary)*

I touch... *(an imaginary touch)*

I worry .... *(something that really bothers you)*

I cry.. *(something that makes you very sad)*

I am........................... *(the first line of the poem repeated)*

3rd Stanza

I understand .... *(something you know is true)*

I say... *(something you believe in)*

I dream....................................... *(something you actually dream about)*

I try.................................. *(something you really make an effort about)*

I hope... *(something you actually hope for)*

I am...................................... *(the first line of the poem repeated)*

Now, write your own poem here:

1st Stanza

I am _____

I wonder _____

I hear _____

I see _____

I want _____

I am _____

2nd Stanza

I pretend _____

I feel _____

I touch _____

I worry _____

I cry _____

I am _____

3rd Stanza

I understand _____

I say _____

I dream _____

I try _____

I hope _____

I am _____

WRITE!

Today's date: _____

DRAW!

Today's date: _____

Which state is home to the Roller Coaster Capital of the World? **Ohio!**

Cedar Point is in Sandusky, Ohio, and it's known as "America's Roller Coast" because it has 17 roller coasters. That's more than any other amusement park in the world!

Now create and draw your own roller coaster!

Things to think about:
- How many hills will it have?
- Will it go upside down?
- How fast do you want it to go?
- How tall do you want it to be?
- What is its name?

What makes YOU an Ohio kid?